SEEDFOLKS

by
Paul Fleischman

Teacher Guide

Written by
Heather M. Marnan

Note

The 2004 Harper Trophy paperback edition of the book, © 1997 by Paul Fleischman, was used to prepare this guide. The page references may differ in other editions. Novel ISBN: 987-0-06-447207-4

Please note: This novel deals with sensitive, mature issues. Parts may contain profanity, sexual references, and/or descriptions of violence. Please assess the appropriateness of this book for the age level and maturity of your students prior to reading and discussing it with them.

ISBN: 978-1-56137-077-1

To order, contact your local school supply store, or—

Table of Contents

Skills and Strategies

Thinking
Predicting, brainstorming, research

Comprehension
Pros/cons, compare/contrast

Writing
Freewriting, poem, letter, essay, fiction, brochure

Listening/Speaking
Discussion with classroom guests, interview

Vocabulary
Synonym, antonym, word map, glossary, word scramble

Literary Elements
Character analysis, story map, conflict, point of view, metaphor, simile

Across the Curriculum
Social Studies—multicultural issues; Art—collage, sketch, caricature; Science—horticulture; Drama—skit; Music—jazz (Miles Davis)

Genre: fiction

Setting: a vacant lot turned garden in modern-day Cleveland

Point of View: first person from 13 different viewpoints

Themes: suspicion, tolerance, community, redemption, hope, new beginnings

Conflict: person vs. person, person vs. self, person vs. nature, person vs. society

Style: narrative

Tone: alternates between despairing and hopeful

Date of First Publication: 1999

Summary

A group of people—different in age, race, culture, and circumstance—resurrect a dirty, vacant lot in their neighborhood. The lot is turned into a garden, and each person contributes in some way, either as a planter or as an observer. Although each person has his/her own story, the garden inadvertently connects the individuals of the neighborhood. The garden soon becomes the focal point of the neighborhood, and the lives of the people participating in its development are forever changed.

About the Author

Paul Fleischman, the son of Newbery Medal-winning author Sid Fleischman, grew up in Santa Monica, California. He attended college at the University of New Mexico and after graduation worked as a bookstore clerk, library shelver, and proofreader. Paul says that "words are my world," and it was this feeling that led him to establish The Society for the Prevention of Cruelty to English, a group dedicated to ensuring the correct use of grammar. He has a passion for history and music—prevalent themes in his novels—as well as theater. He writes many of his novels in a way that allows them to be performed as plays or skits. Paul and his wife have two sons, Seth and Dana, and currently live in Aromas, California. His novel, *Seedfolks*, won the Buckeye Children's Book Award. Some of Paul's other award-winning works include *Bull Run*, winner of the Scott O'Dell Award for Historical Fiction; *Graven Images*, a Newbery Honor book; *A Fate Totally Worse Than Death*, winner of the Children's Choices Award; *Saturnalia*, winner of the Boston Globe-Horn Book Fiction Honor Award; and *Joyful Noise: Poems for Two Voices*, winner of the Newbery Medal. In addition to young-adult fiction and poetry, Paul writes picture books, nonfiction, and plays.

Characters

Kim: nine-year-old Vietnamese girl; first to start the garden; plants bean seeds to please her deceased father

Ana: elderly, nosy, white woman; suspects Kim of burying something illegal in the garden and digs up the bean seeds

Wendell: middle-aged white man; waters Kim's bean seeds after Ana enlists his help; finds hope in the garden

Gonzalo: eighth-grade Guatemalan boy; learns to garden from his uncle

Leona: middle-aged black woman; plans to plant goldenrod in the garden in honor of her grandmother; complains to the city about the trash and foul smells in the garden in hopes of getting it cleaned up

Sam: 78-year-old Jewish man; views the garden as a unifier for the neighborhood

Virgil: fifth-grade Haitian boy; helps his father plant lettuce to sell

Sae Young: middle-aged Korean woman; reclusive after being robbed at gunpoint; uses the garden and its visitors to heal

Curtis: 28-year-old black man; plants tomatoes in hopes of winning his ex-girlfriend's affection

Nora: British woman of indeterminate age; nurse for an infirm black man; helps her patient regain some vitality by assisting him with planting flowers in the garden

Maricela: 16-year-old pregnant Mexican girl; unhappy about her situation; befriends Leona in the garden

Amir: middle-aged man from India; witnesses the garden's power to integrate people and eliminate prejudices

Florence: retired black woman; observes the garden during the changing seasons and hopes that people resume their planting in the spring

Initiating Activities

1. Freewriting: Provide students with the following prompts. Ask each student to choose one and freewrite about it for at least ten minutes. Encourage students to share their writing with the class.

   a. Write about an activity that you have participated in with a diverse group of people, particularly people of different cultures. What was the activity? How did you become involved? Do you still communicate with any of the group members?

   b. Have you ever had a "friend of circumstance"—a person you befriended only because you were both in the same situation or place at the same time? If so, write about the friendship and how it began. If not, write about whether you think it is possible to maintain such a friendship when the instigating circumstances change.

2. Prediction: Have students study the cover, consider the title, and read the text on the first page of the novel. Based on their examination, have students predict what the book will be about. Students may use the Prediction Chart on page 19 of this guide.

3. Brainstorming: Using the Attribute Web (see p. 20 of this guide). Have students brainstorm a list of transformations (e.g., seed to plant, egg to hatchling, infant to adult, etc.) and write these on the long spokes. Then have students determine whether nature, nurture, or both is the cause of each transformation's success and write the responses on the corresponding short spokes of the web.

4. Social Studies: Invite several school faculty and staff members of varying ages, races, and cultures to the class. Lead a discussion that examines how well the school promotes diversity of all kinds. Encourage student participation.

Vocabulary Activities

1. Synonym Survival: Have students stand in a circle. Recite a vocabulary word from the novel, and toss a ball (or other small object) to a student. The student must give a synonym for the word. Keep the ball moving until all synonyms are listed. The class earns one point for each correct synonym given. At the end of the turn, retrieve the ball and start again, reciting a different word. Set a time limit, and challenge the class to earn 15 points by the end of the game. Note: This game can also be played to provide practice with antonyms.

2. Vocabulary Word Map: Have students complete the Vocabulary Word Map on page 21 of this guide for a target word from each section.

3. Definition Diorama: Instruct each student to choose one vocabulary word from the novel and construct a diorama that represents the meaning of the word. Note: You may wish to remind students that nouns and adjectives work best for this activity.

4. Glossary: Have students create a glossary of any difficult or unknown words they encounter while reading the novel.

5. Word Scramble: Have students form groups of three or four. Give each group a collection of paper squares with each square displaying a letter. When the letters are put in the proper order, they form a vocabulary word. The first group to unscramble their word and write the definition on the board wins. Each group should receive a different vocabulary word. Example: a group receives six squares with the letters I L W E T D, which will spell "wilted."

Kim–Wendell

Kim is a young Vietnamese girl whose father died before she was born. Because her father was a farmer, Kim plants lima bean seeds in a vacant lot near her apartment to make her father proud. She hopes the beans will grow so her father will "see" her accomplishment.

Ana likes to watch people in other apartments, and she notices Kim in the vacant lot. She believes Kim is burying something illegal, and she goes to the lot and digs up Kim's seeds. Horrified at her mistake and the ruined plants, Ana reburies the seeds and waters them.

Wendell is not fond of receiving phone calls because of the bad news they almost inevitably bring. He found out about the deaths of his son and wife via telephone. He is not pleased when Ana calls to ask for help to save Kim's dying bean plants. However, he goes to the vacant lot and rescues the plants. Kim sees him and is afraid, but she later imitates his watering methods. Wendell realizes that a garden is one thing in his life he can change and improve. He decides to plant something of his own in the lot.

Vocabulary

altar
stern
incense
gnawing
vowed
thrive
vacant
lad
parole
wilted

Discussion Questions

1. For what does Kim wish as she looks at the photograph of her father? How does Kim perceive her father? *(She wishes her father's eyes would move and look at her. She wants her father to notice her. As evident by her description of the photograph, Kim sees her father as having been a strict, serious man.)*

2. Describe the place where Kim goes to plant her seeds. Why do you suppose Kim chooses this place? *(It is a vacant lot filled with trash and abandoned items. There is an old couch where people can be found sleeping, a rusty refrigerator, and rats that feast on the trash in the lot. Kim is afraid to walk into the lot. Answers will vary.)*

3. How does Kim feel when she thinks of her father? *(She is saddened by the fact that she has no memories of him. She worries that since her father died before she was born, he does not know or recognize her.)*

4. Explain Kim's rationale for planting the bean seeds. *(Kim's father was a farmer, and she wants to grow something to make him proud. She believes that if he sees her plants growing, he will know that she is like him and therefore recognize her as his daughter.)*

5. What does Ana believe Kim is doing in the vacant lot? What does this assumption reveal about Ana's character? *(Ana sees Kim crouched down in the vacant lot and thinks she is burying something illegal. Because Ana watches the goings-on of the city outside her window and sees a lot of mischief, she assumes Kim is doing something wrong. Her assumption shows that she is nosy and suspicious.)*

6. How does Ana discover her mistake regarding Kim's activities? Why do you suppose she reacts this way? *(Ana goes to the vacant lot intending to dig up whatever Kim had buried. When she digs into the soil, she finds the bean seeds and realizes that Kim planted them. Answers will vary but should include that Ana is self-assured and judgmental. She wants to take credit for revealing Kim's unsuitable behavior.)*

7. Why is Wendell angry that Ana calls him? *(He hates phone calls because they always seem to bring him bad news. Ana's phone call awakens him, and she frightens him by demanding that he come to her apartment quickly.)*

8. Why do you suppose Kim is afraid when she sees Wendell? Why doesn't Wendell speak to her? *(Answers will vary.)*

9. Analyze Wendell's statement: "Better to put my time into [changing the lot] than moaning about the other all day" (p. 15). *(Wendell has had a lot of heartache in his life and so has become pessimistic and cynical. However, seeing Kim work in the vacant lot, he realizes that he can make something in his life better—even if it is only a small area of soil—instead of complaining about everything else.)*

Supplementary Activities

1. Literary Devices: Discuss the author's use of similes and metaphors throughout the novel. Use the Metaphors and Similes chart on page 22 of this guide to keep a list of literary devices as you read the book.

2. Literary Analysis: Begin a Story Map like the one on page 23 of this guide. You may use your own paper for this activity, which will continue as you read the novel.

3. Art: Sketch one of the following: (a) Kim's family altar (b) Ana's view of the vacant lot (c) the area of the lot where Kim has planted her seeds.

4. Research: Research effective watering methods for small vegetables, such as lima beans. Create either a poster or brochure showing proper instructions for the care of small vegetable plants.

Gonzalo–Leona

Gonzalo lives with his Spanish-speaking family in an apartment near the vacant lot. He feels as though he has become the adult and his parents have become like children, since they cannot speak English and are unable to function on a daily basis. He is placed in charge of his uncle and one day notices him missing. His uncle has gone to the vacant lot and is trying to help Wendell with his planting. Gonzalo is embarrassed, but he later sees how being in the garden makes his uncle very happy.

Leona plans to plant goldenrod in the vacant lot to honor her deceased grandmother. When she notices how dirty and smelly the vacant lot is, she begins making phone calls to have someone clean up the lot. After many phone calls with no results, Leona decides to meet someone in person in hopes of achieving her goal. She visits the health department with a bag of trash from the vacant lot. The smell of the garbage gets the desired results; Leona convinces the city to clean the vacant lot so neighborhood residents can use it as a garden.

Vocabulary
equation
bodega
pueblo
gestures
trowel
troughs
citizens
maggots
receptionist

Discussion Questions

1. How did Gonzalo learn to speak English? (*He learned English on the playground and from watching TV, especially cartoons.*)

2. How does Gonzalo feel about his father and uncle? Why does he feel this way? (*He believes both men have become like babies again since arriving in the United States. Since neither man can speak English, both are practically helpless and depend on Gonzalo to perform everyday functions for them. He feels as though this makes him the adult, while his father and uncle have reverted to being children.*)

3. What happens to Gonzalo's uncle? Where does he go? (*Gonzalo's uncle wanders away from the apartment, and Gonzalo cannot find him. He goes into the vacant lot, where Gonzalo finds him trying to communicate with Wendell.*)

4. How does Gonzalo's uncle react upon reentering the vacant lot? (*He is very excited about being there. He looks at the sun. He feels, smells, and tastes the soil. In contrast to when he begins planting the seeds, he is extremely focused and aware.*)

5. Why do you suppose Gonzalo's uncle is able to be happy when in the vacant lot? (*Answers will vary but should include that he does not feel pressured to speak, so his language inadequacies are not evident. He knows about planting seeds, so he feels confident instead of childish.*)

6. What is Leona's problem with the vacant lot? How does she intend to solve this problem? (*She is concerned about the amount of trash in the lot, as well as the awful smells. Leona plans to call city officials and ask them to clean up the lot.*)

7. What is Leona's ultimate realization about the vacant lot? What does she do? Do you agree with her actions? Why or why not? (*Leona realizes that no one will pay attention to her as long as she is just using the telephone. She visits the health department and brings along a bag of smelly trash from the lot, forcing people to notice and listen to her. Answers will vary.*)

Supplementary Activities

1. Literary Devices: **Similes**—"So he wandered around...just like a kid in diapers" (p. 19); "He seemed to recognize them, like old friends" (p. 22).

2. Social Studies: Research a local program designed to teach English to Spanish-speaking citizens. If none exists locally, research another assimilation program in your area.

3. Social Studies: Interview a local city official. Ask questions about the official's duties, what area of the city he or she is responsible for, and how he or she achieves his/her goals. Write a brief report on your interview, or give an oral presentation to the class.

4. Music: Leona listens to Miles Davis while she calls government offices. Find and listen to music by Miles Davis. Then, write a response to the music including your opinion of the music, why you think Leona would play it while on the phone, and how playing such music might help you in your own life.

Sam–Virgil

Sam is an older man who believes in peace and integration. He views the garden as a means for uniting individuals in the neighborhood. However, even as he sees the garden's ability to transform, Sam witnesses hatred and division among the people in the garden.

Virgil is a young boy whose father, a taxi cab driver, has decided to grow lettuce for profit. Virgil and his father take a large portion of the garden for themselves, lying that it is for other people who cannot attend the garden. They work very hard planting the lettuce, but to no avail. The lettuce plants grow crookedly, the leaves wilt, and bugs destroy the plants. Virgil's father is upset that his plan is not working, and Virgil is angry with his father for failing.

Vocabulary
herring
occupation
pacifism
compromised
spigot
crowning
pecking
plantation
myths
goddess

Discussion Questions

1. What does Sam think of when he sees the men clearing the vacant lot? Why does he think this? (*He thinks of the word "paradise." The word originates from a Persian word meaning "walled park," and Sam thinks the garden inside the vacant lot is beautiful.*)

2. According to Sam, what are the main problems in the garden? (*#1—There is no water in the garden; it has to be brought in from other places. #2—The garden eventually becomes segregated, with each group of people gardening next to people of their own nationality/race. #3—People still throw trash in the garden. #4—People fight and add fencing in their areas of the garden to keep others out.*)

3. Why does Virgil's father wake him up early the morning after school is out? What is he planning to do? (*Virgil's father brings him to the garden, and they prepare six spots for planting. They sift through the soil, clearing the trash. Virgil's father wants to plant lettuce to sell to restaurants for profit.*)

4. What does Virgil find while clearing his spots in the garden? How is this item significant? (*a locket with a picture of a woman inside; Later, when their lettuce is dying, Virgil asks the woman to save their plants because she resembles the Greek goddess of crops and the earth.*)

5. What embarrasses Virgil after he and his father plant the lettuce? *(Miss Fleck, Virgil's third-grade teacher, inquires about the size of their garden. Virgil is embarrassed that they have taken up so much space and even more so when his father lies to Miss Fleck about the reason for it.)*

6. What is the outcome of Virgil's father's plan to make money from the lettuce plants? How does this make Virgil and his father feel? *(The lettuce plants grow crookedly, the leaves wilt, and bugs begin eating the plants. Virgil's father is devastated and desperate to save the plants. Virgil is angry with his father for failing and disappointed that he will not be able to buy a new bike.)*

Supplementary Activities

1. Literary Devices: **Similes**—"like a cat who smells herring" (p. 29); "soil…flowed through your fingers like silk" (p. 31); "Water is heavy as bricks" (p. 32); "a bottle came down, like a meteor" (p. 34); "picking out broken glass, like chickens pecking seeds" (p. 38); "like having a new baby in the family" (p. 42)

2. Art: Create a collage that depicts your interpretation of paradise. You may create their own illustrations or use pictures cut out of magazines or newspapers to make your collage. Your teacher will display the collages in the classroom.

3. Science/Research: Research the crop in your state. In a brief essay, have students answer the following questions: What is the crop? What conditions are necessary to grow it? What is the state's annual revenue for this crop? You may also wish to discuss the likelihood of an individual, like Virgil's father, profiting from a small, personal garden.

Sae Young–Curtis

Sae Young is a Korean woman who moved to America with her husband to open a dry cleaning shop. Her husband dies of a heart attack at an early age and Sae Young is left to run the business. She is attacked and robbed at gunpoint, which makes her fearful of people and unable to leave her apartment. After visiting the garden, Sae Young begins to feel happy again and is not afraid. She likes to be with people while they work and even takes part in bringing water into the garden by buying funnels for easier pouring. When she notices people using her funnels, Sae Young is happy and peaceful.

Curtis is a self-centered young man who has lost his girlfriend Lateesha because of his flirtations with other women. After he matures, he decides to grow tomato plants in the garden in hopes of winning her affection because he knows that she loves to eat tomatoes. He takes care of the plants every day, even asking an intimidating homeless black boy to protect the plants at night. Lateesha notices the plants, but Curtis is still unsure if his plan will work.

Vocabulary
alterations
interrupt
spouts
pecs
deeds
blight
fertilizer
sharecropper
billiard

Discussion Questions

1. What happens to Sae Young after she moves to America? *(She and her husband open a dry cleaning shop. Her husband dies, leaving her to run the shop alone. One day she is attacked and robbed at gunpoint, causing her to stay in her apartment and be afraid of everyone.)*

2. How does the garden help Sae Young? *(When she is in the garden, Sae Young is not afraid of people. She feels happy, safe, and eager to talk to people.)*

3. Sae Young correctly identifies Kim's nationality, unlike Wendell. Why do you suppose this is so? *(Answers will vary but should include that since Sae Young is Korean, she is more likely to know about Vietnamese people and also to be sensitive to the differences between Asian groups.)*

4. Briefly describe the contest that Sam hosts. How does Sae Young contribute? How does this make her feel? *(Sam hosts a contest for the children in the garden; they are to devise a solution for bringing water into the garden. The people in the garden will implement the winning idea. Sae Young contributes by buying funnels to make it easier for people to pour water from the containers. She feels glad when she sees people using the funnels, like she belongs there.)*

5. Why did Lateesha, Curtis' girlfriend, leave him? How does he intend to win her back? *(She caught him with another girl. Curtis plans to plant tomatoes, Lateesha's favorite food, in the garden directly under her apartment window.)*

6. How does Curtis treat his tomato plants? How do others respond to this? *(Curtis likes to be in the garden, and he tends to his plants daily. People on the street call him derogatory names, and his friends harass him for being in the garden.)*

7. Whom does Curtis ask to protect his tomato plants? How does this person honor Curtis' request? *(Royce, a formidable teenage boy; Royce sleeps in the garden near Curtis' tomato plants. He holds a pitchfork and chases after anyone trying to mess with Curtis' plants.)*

8. Analyze Royce's statement: "If people know something belongs to a person instead of the city or the U.S. government they're more likely to leave it be" (p. 58). Do you agree with this statement? Why or why not? Cite specific examples to justify your response. *(Answers will vary.)*

Supplementary Activities

1. Literary Devices: **Similes**—"sound of people working…like conversation" (p. 48); "[tomatoes] bright as traffic lights" (p. 53); "[Lateesha's face] as still as a cat" (p. 58)

2. Characterization: Complete the Feelings chart on page 24 of this guide for Sae Young.

3. Poetry: Write an acrostic love poem (in which a word is written vertically and each letter of a word forms the first letter of each line) from Curtis' point of view using one of the following words: tomato, Lateesha, redemption, garden, deltoid.

Nora–Maricela

Nora is British woman who works as a nurse for an ailing elderly man named Mr. Myles. A stroke has left him unable to speak and without much vitality. One day, as Nora is walking with Mr. Myles in his wheelchair, he motions for her to stop near the garden. She is surprised at this, because Mr. Myles is usually unmoved by the world during their walks. Seeing him show interest in the people planting, Nora decides to bring him back to the garden, crafting a pot out of a barrel so that Mr. Myles may plant flowers from his wheelchair. Nora is amazed at the garden's ability to bring so many different people together.

Maricela is a 16-year-old pregnant Mexican girl. She is very unhappy about her situation and often wishes that both she and her unborn child were dead. After joining a support group for pregnant teens, Maricela visits the garden at the insistence of the group's director. She dislikes the garden immensely and cannot stop thinking of ways to harm her unborn child to relieve herself of her perceived burden. However, Maricela speaks with Leona in the garden and soon finds herself thinking of more positive things. She feels as though she is part of something important and momentarily believes that her life may not be over after all.

Note to Teachers: The section regarding Maricela's story contains sensitive material some students may find uncomfortable (e.g., the pregnant character mentions her desire for a miscarriage in multiple forms throughout the chapter).

Vocabulary
prams
gales
dignified
obliged
domestic
entranced
tremolo
furrowed
pantomime
notion
chard
decorum
disgrace

Discussion Questions

1. What does Mr. Myles do when he and Nora pass the garden? Why does this surprise Nora? (*He raises his arm, motioning for Nora to stop. Nora is surprised because Mr. Myles is an ailing old man who does not respond to much anymore. He is practically lifeless most days, so Nora is surprised when he shows interest in the garden.*)

2. How does Nora help Mr. Myles participate in the garden? What does this say about her character? (*She fills a barrel with soil so Mr. Myles can plant flowers from his wheelchair without having to get on the ground. This shows that Nora is a kind and thoughtful person. She is eager to help Mr. Myles do something he enjoys, even though it means hard work for her.*)

3. What effect does the garden have on Nora? on Mr. Myles? (*Nora feels excitement and anticipation when she is in the garden. She is amazed at how the garden transforms Mr. Myles. Although he does not speak, Mr. Myles is obviously happy. His face regains its vitality, and he is satisfied with the flowers he plants.*)

4. How does Maricela feel about herself? Why does she feel this way? *(She is not happy with herself at all. Because she is a pregnant Mexican teenager, she thinks she is not worthy of living. She hates the way her body looks, dropped out of school, and wishes terrible things would happen to her and her unborn child.)*

5. Why does Maricela visit the garden? How does she feel about this? *(She is a member of a program for pregnant teenagers, and her program director has made visiting the garden part of the program. Maricela and the other girls are supposed to grow different plants to get accustomed to taking care of something. Maricela hates the garden, the other girls in her group, and the way people talk to her.)*

6. To whom does Maricela speak in the garden? What does this person tell her? *(Leona; that Maricela is part of nature and its systems, and it is an honor to be so)*

7. How does Maricela feel as a result of her conversation with Leona? Do you think Maricela will continue to feel this way? *(Maricela listens and enjoys talking to Leona. She feels momentarily better about her situation; Answers will vary.)*

Supplementary Activities

1. Literary Devices: **Similes**—"slam on the brakes like the Pope just stepped in front of him" (p. 70); **Metaphors**—Mr. Myles: a mystery (p. 60), a salmon traveling upstream (p. 61); small circle of earth: a second home (p. 63); gardening: a soap opera, a mind-altering drug (p. 63)

2. Research: Research the therapeutic effects of certain outdoor activities (e.g., gardening). Create a poster displaying your results and display the posters in the classroom.

3. Research: Maricela's group gardens to learn about responsibility and how to care for something. Research different methods used to prepare first-time mothers for the responsibilities of childcare. Create either a poster or brochure that lists these methods, and write a one-page paper about which methods would work best for Maricela.

Amir–Florence

Amir is an Indian man who owns a fabric store. He plants vegetables in the garden and marvels at the attention his crops bring. He notices that people who would otherwise be ill at ease with each other are transformed into immediate friends while in the garden. Amir enjoys the festive feel of the garden, and he participates willingly in the harvest party held there. After amicably speaking with a woman who had previously been rude to him at his store, Amir decides that the garden has the power to make people really see each other instead of the stereotypes so often assumed.

Florence likes to watch the people in the garden. Although she cannot participate in the planting because of arthritis in her hands, she walks by the garden daily and protects it as though it were her own. After planting season is over, Florence watches the garden change with the seasons, hoping all the while that the planters return in the spring. When the winter is over, Florence is pleased when she sees Kim in the garden, once again planting her lima bean seeds.

Vocabulary
vast
foes
eerie
exploit
spit
homesteaded
arthritis
sampler
idle

Discussion Questions

1. How does Amir compare and contrast India and America? Do you agree with his assumption? Why or why not? (*He says that both countries have many cities and many people. However, he believes that people in America do not wish to be friends with each other, as they do in India. Answers will vary.*)

2. In what ways does the garden change Amir's opinion about the neighborhood? (*While in the garden, people are friendly and speak to Amir freely. The people in the garden unite to help and protect one another. Amir knows that most of this would not take place outside the garden, but he is still amazed at how easily everyone gets along.*)

3. How are Amir's own stereotypical beliefs challenged in the garden? (*He speaks with a Polish woman, who contradicts everything Amir has ever heard or believed about Polish people. Amir becomes acquainted with and grows to trust Royce, whom he would otherwise have feared and avoided.*)

4. Whom does Amir meet at the barbecue? How does he react? How does the other person respond? How would you have reacted in his situation? (*a woman who previously called him a derogatory name in his store; Amir confronts her about the incident, and she apologizes. She justifies her actions by claiming she would not have done it had she known it was Amir. Answers will vary.*)

5. Why does Florence appreciate the garden so much? (*She grew up in the country, and she misses "country things."*)

6. What happens to the garden during the fall? How does this make Florence feel? (*The garden turns brown, and the people leave. All of the color is gone from the garden. This saddens Florence, who likes to watch the people tend to their plants in the garden.*)

7. What is Florence's greatest fear about the garden? Why do you suppose this worries her so much? (*She is afraid that no one will return in the spring to plant the garden again. Answers will vary but should include that Florence derives great pleasure in seeing the garden, as it reminds her of where she grew up.*)

Supplementary Activities

1. Literary Devices: **Similes**—"like the worthless shell around an almond" (p. 77); "Waiting for the snow to melt was like waiting for a glacier to move" (p. 86–87); "like a bookmark showing where you'd left off" (p. 87); **Metaphors**—Americans: crabs (p. 73); Persian rugs: portable gardens (p. 74)

2. Writing: Write about a time when you were discriminated against. How did you handle this incident? Was the incident amicably resolved? If so, how?

3. Art: Create illustration of the garden in fall. Use Florence's description of the garden on pages 85–86 of the novel as a basis for your illustration.

Afterword: From Seed to Seedfolks

The author offers his thoughts on writers and writing techniques. He presents the process for *Seedfolks'* creation, as well as his belief in the importance of community gardens.

Note to Teachers:

As the Afterword is merely a narrative from the author, you may wish to omit this section from your novel study. However, there are many words in this section that lend themselves to effective vocabulary study, and these words have been included in this guide. Likewise, if your students are completing the Metaphor and Simile chart (Section 1, Supplementary Activity #1, p. 7 of this guide), examples of these literary devices have been given below.

Vocabulary
affliction
serendipity
tabloid
camaraderie
monologues
aversion
presaging
baron
propagation
vigilance
aria
invective
pillaging
waived
solace
altruism
potent

Discussion Questions

1. How did the author get the idea for Seedfolks? *(random accident; from reading a New Age tabloid article about a psychiatrist using gardening as a healing tool)*

2. How does the author compare writers and gardeners? *(both tend to be self-taught and value self-sufficiency)*

3. What does the author mean when he says using an idea that is ready-made is like "buying a house that's already furnished" (p. 95). *(Answers will vary.)*

Supplementary Activities

1. Literary Devices: **Similes**—"like buying a house that's already furnished" (p. 95); "like sailors awaiting a ship" (p. 97); "Books are...like seeds" (p. 100); **Metaphor**—community gardens: oases (p. 102)

Post-reading Discussion Questions

1. Which character(s) do you believe will most likely continue visiting the garden? Give specific reasons to support your answer. *(Answers will vary.)*

2. Which characters do you believe experience the greatest transformation? Explain your answer. *(Answers will vary.)*

3. In what ways is the community garden a symbol of hope for the neighborhood? *(Answers will vary, as the garden becomes a symbol of hope for all of the characters. Suggestions: By visiting the garden, Sae Young is able to rejoin society after her fateful attack. Maricela finds herself thinking of something other than her pregnancy when she is in the garden. Nora notices that Mr. Myles seems livelier when he is in the garden.)*

4. Would you recommend this novel to a friend? Why or why not? *(Answers will vary.)*

5. How would the tone of the novel have been different if the individuals in the neighborhood were members of the same culture? Do you believe the story would have been better or worse? *(The tone possibly would have been more upbeat, since there would not have been as many judgments made, suspicions aroused, and prejudices revealed. However, if the characters were from the same background, the author would not have been able to convey the importance of the garden to so many different people for so many different reasons. The garden would have been a much weaker symbol of togetherness. Answers will vary.)*

6. Discuss the differences between the ages of the characters and their reactions to the garden. *(The younger characters, such as Kim, Gonzalo, and Curtis, are extremely optimistic about the garden and its effects. With the exception of Maricela, the younger characters are confident that their activities in the garden will bring about happiness and success in a specific endeavor. The older characters, such as Ana, Wendell, Sam, Amir, and Florence, enjoy the garden but have an underlying feeling of negativity about its ability to create happiness. Leona, Sae Young, and Nora are able to consider the garden in an uplifting manner, even though their personal circumstances are not necessarily promising.)*

7. If you could change one thing about the novel, what would it be and why? *(Answers will vary.)*

8. Examine the role of chance in each character's discovery of the garden. *(Examples: Ana has a habit of looking at the goings-on of the neighborhood with binoculars. She happens to spot Kim planting her bean seeds in the garden. Nora is walking with Mr. Myles and intends to pass the garden, but Mr. Myles stops her with a surprising movement of his arm. Maricela has no desire to be a part of the garden, but her support program requires it.)*

9. Have you ever known someone similar to any of the characters in the novel? If so, describe that person. Which character does s/he resemble and in what way(s)? If not, describe a character from a well-known movie that resembles one of the novel's characters. *(Answers will vary.)*

10. Discuss the universality of the prejudices encountered in this novel. *(Answers will vary but should include the issues of assumptions, judging on first impressions, intolerance, bigotry, and stereotypes.)*

Post-reading Extension Activities

1. Write three or four paragraphs that extend the story of Curtis and his tomato plants. Describe whether he succeeds in winning Lateesha's affection.

2. Using the graphic on page 25 of this guide, sort the characters in the novel.

3. Write a poem about how Gonzalo's uncle feels when he is planting his seeds in the garden.

4. Using magazine photographs, text, and your own illustrations, create a collage depicting one of the character's experiences with the garden.

5. Draw a caricature of Miss Fleck as described by Virgil (see pp. 40–42 of the novel).

6. Research neighborhood organizations in your city aimed at protecting citizens or preserving some aspect of their neighborhoods. Create a classroom chart listing each organization and its purpose.

7. Interview a local gardener or horticulture expert. Be sure to include questions about the best time of year to grow certain plants, as well as the best terrain and most favorable conditions.

8. Complete the Characters With or Without Character chart on page 26 of this guide.

9. Using the word "Transform" to create an acrostic poem that describes the positive effects the neighborhood garden has on the characters in the novel.

Assessment for *Seedfolks*

Assessment is an ongoing process. The following ten items can be completed during the novel study. Once finished, the student and teacher will check the work. Points may be added to indicate the level of understanding.

Name _____ Date _____

Student　　**Teacher**

_____　　_____　　1. Identify a conflict from the novel. Evaluate how the conflict is handled and ultimately resolved by the characters.

_____　　_____　　2. Analyze the pros and cons of participating in a community garden. You may use the chart on page 27 of this guide.

_____　　_____　　3. Choose and research one crop you would grow if you had a garden, and create a step-by-step guide to growing your crop.

_____　　_____　　4. Write another chapter for the novel in which you describe one character's life during the winter after his/her discovery of the garden.

_____　　_____　　5. Describe Kim from Ana's and Wendell's points of view. Compare and contrast the descriptions.

_____　　_____　　6. Select a character and write a bio-poem using the graphic on page 28 of this guide.

_____　　_____　　7. Complete the Character Attribute Web on page 29 of this guide.

_____　　_____　　8. Write a letter to Maricela in which you encourage her to continue visiting the garden and offer advice of other activities that may help her.

_____　　_____　　9. Perform a classroom skit of the scene in which Leona visits the Public Health Department (see p. 28 of the novel).

_____　　_____　　10. Write a short poem about how Lateesha might feel as she looks out her window at Curtis' tomato plants.

Prediction Chart

What characters have we met so far?	What is the conflict in the story?	What are your predictions?	Why did you make these predictions?

Attribute Web

Directions: Use this web to list different kinds of transformations (on the long spokes) and of the transformations, success is the cause of nature or nurture (on the short spokes), and explain why.

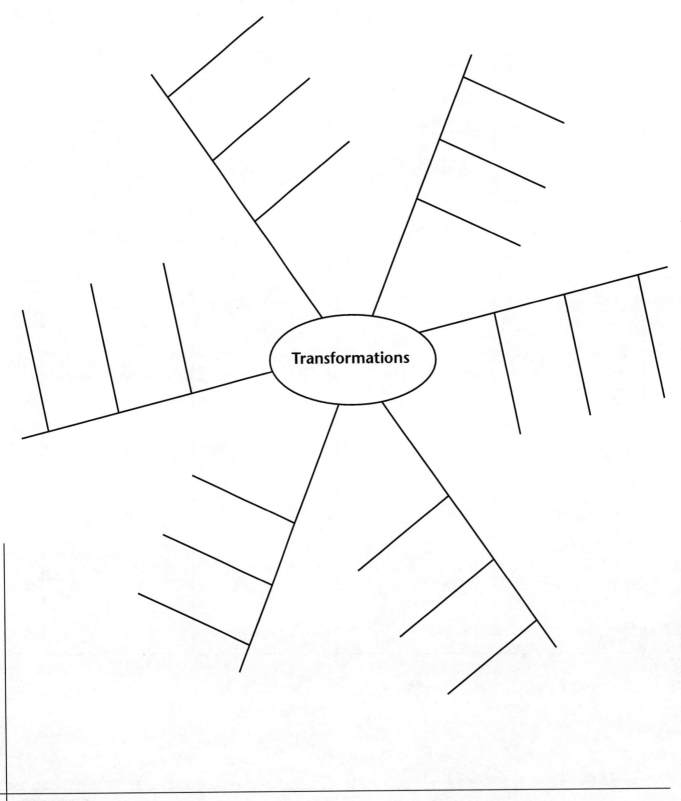

Vocabulary Word Map

Synonyms	Antonyms
_____	_____
_____	_____
_____	_____

WORD

_____

Definition in your own words	Used in a sentence
_____	_____
_____	_____
_____	_____

Metaphors and Similes

A **metaphor** is a comparison between two unlike objects. For example, "he was a human tree." A **simile** is a comparison between two unlike objects that uses the words *like* or *as*. For example, "the color of her eyes was like the cloudless sky."

Directions: Complete the chart below by listing metaphors and similes from the novel, as well as the page numbers on which they are found. Identify metaphors with an "M" and similes with an "S." Translate the comparisons in your own words, and then list the objects being compared.

Metaphors/Similes	Ideas/Objects Being Compared
1. Translation:	
2. Translation:	
3. Translation:	

Story Map

Directions: Use this story map as an example, and create your own story map as you read *Seedfolks*.

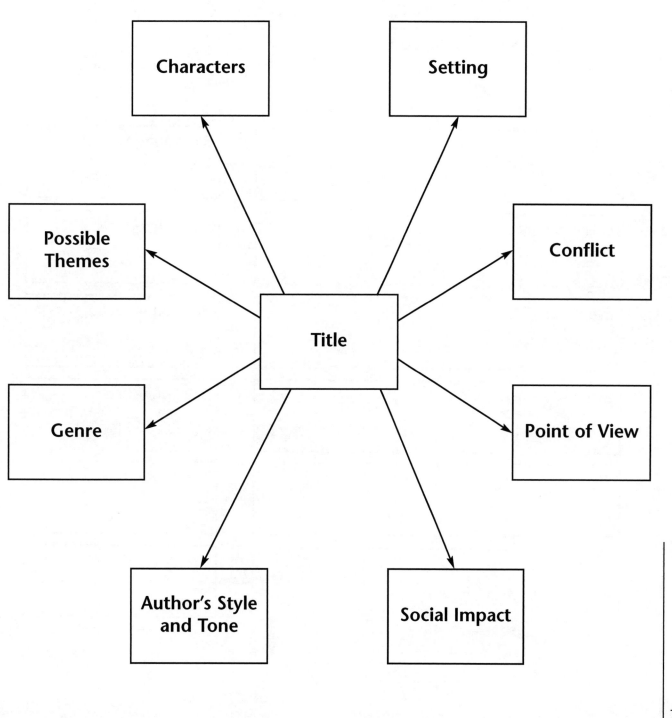

Feelings

Directions: Complete this feelings chart for Sae Young.

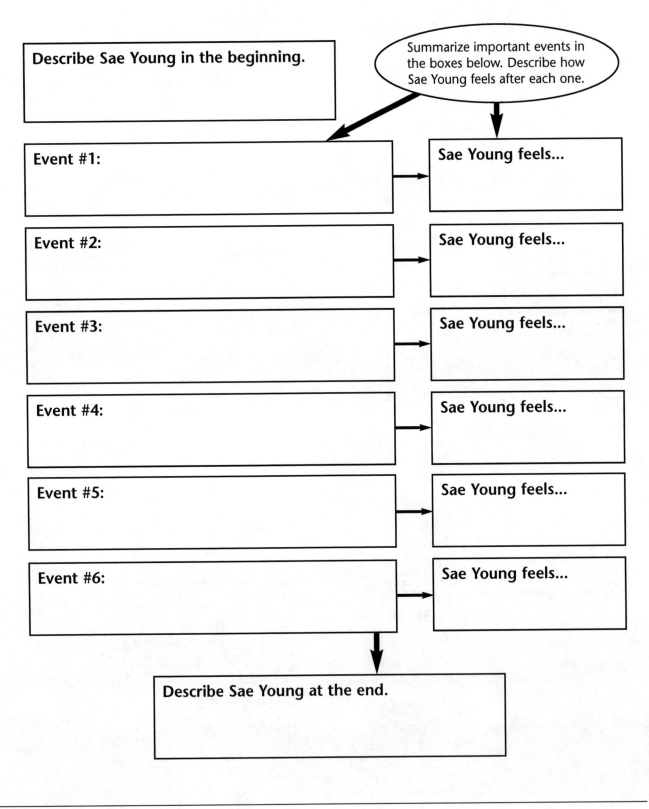

Describe Sae Young in the beginning.

Summarize important events in the boxes below. Describe how Sae Young feels after each one.

Event #1:

Sae Young feels...

Event #2:

Sae Young feels...

Event #3:

Sae Young feels...

Event #4:

Sae Young feels...

Event #5:

Sae Young feels...

Event #6:

Sae Young feels...

Describe Sae Young at the end.

Sorting Characters

Directions: Similarities between characters are sometimes a clue to themes in a story. Write this book's characters in one or more of the groups below.

Victims	Victimizers	Fighters
Peace-lovers	**Conformists**	**Self-directors**

Characters With or Without Character

Character is evaluated by one's actions, statements, and by the way one treats others.

Directions: For each of the attributes listed in the center of the page, write the name of one character from the novel who has this trait and the name of one character who does **not** have this trait. After each character's name, give an example of an action or statement that proves you have properly evaluated the character.

Yes   ### No

Name: _____	Name: _____
Proof: _____	Proof: _____
_____	_____
_____	_____

Is a good person

Name: _____	Name: _____
Proof: _____	Proof: _____
_____	_____
_____	_____

Sacrifices for others

Name: _____	Name: _____
Proof: _____	Proof: _____
_____	_____
_____	_____

Is kind and caring

Pros and Cons

Directions: Write the pros and cons of participating in a community garden.

Bio-poem

Directions: Using the format below, write a bio-poem about a character from the book. Then write a bio-poem about yourself using the same format. Write a paragraph describing the values and characteristics you share.

—Line 1: First name only
—Line 2: Lover of (list three things character loves)
—Line 3: Giver of (list three things character gives)
—Line 4: Needs (list three things character needs)
—Line 5: Wants (list three things character wants)
—Line 6: Is good at (list three things character is good at)
—Line 7: Should work on (list three things character needs to improve)
—Line 8: Is similar to (list three people or other characters to whom this character is similar and list a reason behind each character)
—Line 9: Survivor of (list three things the character survives)
—Line 10: Last name only

Title _____

1. _____

2. _____

3. _____

4. _____

5. _____

6. _____

7. _____

8. _____

9. _____

10. _____

Character Attribute Web

Directions: The attribute web below will help you gather clues the author provides about a character in the novel. Fill in the blanks with words and phrases that tell how the character acts and looks, as well as what the character says and feels.

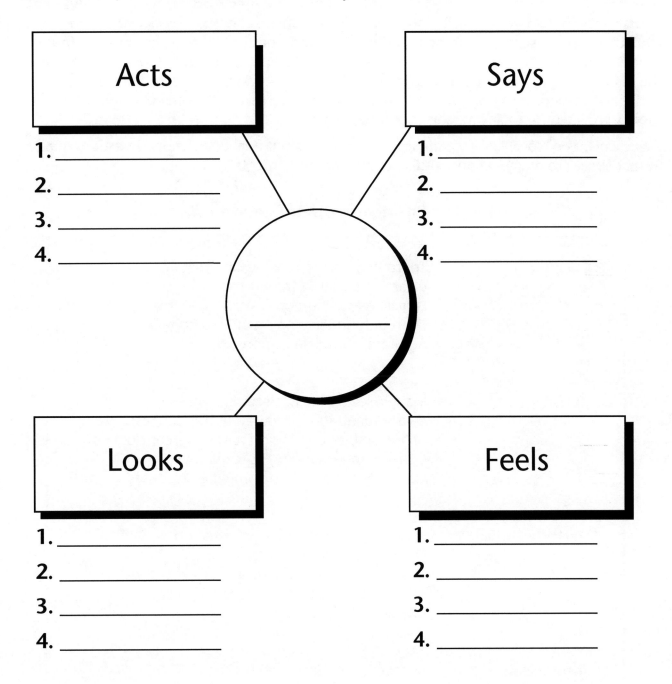

Linking Novel Units® Lessons to National and State Reading Assessments

During the past several years, an increasing number of students have faced some form of state-mandated competency testing in reading. Many states now administer state-developed assessments to measure the skills and knowledge emphasized in their particular reading curriculum. The discussion questions and post-reading questions in this Novel Units® Teacher Guide make excellent open-ended comprehension questions and may be used throughout the daily lessons as practice activities. The rubric below provides important information for evaluating responses to open-ended comprehension questions. Teachers may also use scoring rubrics provided for their own state's competency test.

Please note: The Novel Units® Student Packet contains optional open-ended questions in a format similar to many national and state reading assessments.

Scoring Rubric for Open-Ended Items

3-Exemplary
Thorough, complete ideas/information
Clear organization throughout
Logical reasoning/conclusions
Thorough understanding of reading task
Accurate, complete response

2-Sufficient
Many relevant ideas/pieces of information
Clear organization throughout most of response
Minor problems in logical reasoning/conclusions
General understanding of reading task
Generally accurate and complete response

1-Partially Sufficient
Minimally relevant ideas/information
Obvious gaps in organization
Obvious problems in logical reasoning/conclusions
Minimal understanding of reading task
Inaccuracies/incomplete response

0-Insufficient
Irrelevant ideas/information
No coherent organization
Major problems in logical reasoning/conclusions
Little or no understanding of reading task
Generally inaccurate/incomplete response

Notes

Notes